Wealth That Endures:

The Five-Fold Millionaire's Guide to Lasting Abundance

Dr. Jacquelyn Hadnot
Igniting the Fire Publishing

Copyright 2024 @Dr. Jacquelyn Hadnot

Wealth that Endures: The Five-Fold Millionaires Guide to Lasting Abundance

No part of this publication may be reproduced, stored in a retrieval system, or transmitted, in any form or by any means, electronic, mechanical, photocopying, recording, or otherwise, without the written prior permission of the author.

Used by permission.

Cover Design: Dr. Jacquelyn Hadnot

Copyright© 2024 by Dr. Jacquelyn Hadnot

All rights reserved.

Table of Contents

Introduction	5
1 What is Sustainable Wealth?	9
2 Sustainable Wealth: The Heart of the Five-Fold Millionaire	15
3 How Can I Build Sustainable Wealth?	23
4 Mindset & Attitude	31
5 Building Wealth 1$ at a Time	35
6 Practical Steps	41
7 Time to Move Forward & Build Wealth	47
About the Author	49
Books by Dr. Jacquie	53

Wealth that Endures: The Five-Fold Millionaire's Guide to Lasting Abundance

Introduction

Why write a booklet about a book? Here's my reason. After I finished *The Five-Fold Millionaire*, I realized I hadn't touched on something important—**sustainable wealth**.

Anyone who wants to achieve Five-Fold Millionaire status needs to understand what it really means to have wealth that lasts. Without that, you'll end up broke, frustrated, and wondering where it all went.

My aim in writing *The Five-Fold Millionaire* was to show you how to build wealth, but I also want to make sure you know how to **keep** it, **grow** it, and **pass it on**. It's one thing to acquire wealth, but it's something entirely different to sustain it and create a lasting legacy.

That's why I wrote this booklet—to explain sustainable wealth and why it should be part of your wealth-building toolkit.

Wealth that Endures: The Five-Fold Millionaire's Guide to Lasting Abundance

Wealth That Endures:

The Five-Fold Millionaire's Guide to Lasting Abundance

Dr. Jacquelyn Hadnot
Igniting the Fire Publishing

Wealth that Endures: The Five-Fold Millionaire's
Guide to Lasting Abundance

CHAPTER 1
What is Sustainable Wealth?

Sustainable wealth is all about building, keeping, and growing your money over time, making sure it lasts and provides long-term security. It's not about getting rich quick or having money that comes and goes. Instead, it's about creating a solid financial foundation that can weather the ups and downs of life—whether it's changes in the economy, personal setbacks, or other unexpected challenges.

But here's the thing—sustainable wealth isn't just about money. It's about taking care of your health, nurturing your relationships, and finding fulfillment in life. True wealth goes beyond your bank account. It's about building a life that's rich in every sense of the word.

Here's a breakdown of what it means to have sustainable wealth:

1. **Long-term financial stability** is about making smart money moves that last. Sustainable wealth means planning, saving, and investing wisely. It's about setting up multiple streams of income whether through investments, businesses, real estate, or other assets that grow over time. The focus isn't on getting rich fast, but on making sure your wealth supports you throughout your life and can even be passed on to future generations.

2. **Debt Management and Cash Flow**: Managing debt wisely is a crucial part of sustainable wealth. This means keeping bad debt (the kind that doesn't bring in money) to a minimum, while using good debt (like investing in a business or property) to help grow

your wealth. It's also important to maintain a steady cash flow. That way, you can cover your bills, invest in new opportunities, and have a safety net for those unexpected emergencies.

3. **Asset Protection and Risk Management**: To make sure your wealth lasts, it's crucial to protect your assets with the right legal and financial tools. This might include insurance, trusts, or a will to shield against risks like lawsuits, accidents, market swings, or unexpected events. By protecting what you've built, you can keep your wealth secure and sustainable, even when life throws challenges your way.

4. **Balanced Wealth**: Sustainable wealth isn't just about money—it's about being rich in all areas of life: spiritual, mental, emotional, and physical. These pieces all work together to help you live a balanced and fulfilled life, making sure that financial success

doesn't come at the cost of your health or happiness. For example, taking care of your physical health gives you the energy to actually enjoy your wealth. And when you're emotionally and mentally strong, you can make better financial decisions and handle stress more effectively.

5. **Social Responsibility and Legacy**: Sustainable wealth often means giving back and making a difference in the world. This could be through philanthropy, running your business responsibly, or creating opportunities for others. Many people with lasting wealth focus on leaving a legacy—not just in money, but in the impact they have. Whether it's starting a charitable foundation, mentoring others, or supporting causes that match their values, they aim to make their wealth matter beyond just themselves.

6. **Continual Learning and Growth**: The world of finance is always

shifting, and building sustainable wealth means staying open to learning and adapting. Those who achieve lasting wealth are usually the ones who keep up with economic trends, smart investments, and new opportunities. They also focus on personal growth, developing skills, knowledge, and connections that help enrich both their lives and their financial success.

7. **Intergenerational Wealth Transfer**: Sustainable wealth means planning carefully for how your money will be passed down to future generations. This might involve estate planning, teaching your heirs how to manage money wisely, and putting systems in place to make sure the wealth isn't wasted. By doing this, you help preserve your wealth so that it can support not only your family now, but also future generations to come.

In the journey toward sustainable wealth, think of it like building a house. You start with a strong foundation—one built on smart financial decisions that last a lifetime. It's not just about making money quickly but about laying the groundwork for long-term security.

As you move forward, you carefully construct the walls, making sure to protect what you've built. This might be through managing risks, insuring your assets, or making sure your wealth is passed down wisely to future generations.

Chapter 2
Sustainable Wealth: The Heart of the Five-Fold Millionaire

Sustainable wealth and the idea of a five-fold millionaire are intricately connected. Both focus on achieving lasting prosperity that isn't just about money. Here's how these two concepts come together:

1. Balanced Approach to Wealth:
- The five-fold millionaire looks at wealth from five different angles: spiritual, mental, emotional, physical, and financial. It understands that real abundance includes much more than just having money. In the same way, sustainable wealth takes this wider

view, highlighting how essential it is to focus on well-being in all areas of life to build a solid and lasting foundation for success.

- For instance, spiritual wealth means aligning your purpose with your financial goals, making sure your success has a positive impact on your life and the world around you. Emotional wealth helps you stay mentally and emotionally balanced, allowing you to make smart financial decisions and face challenges effectively.

2. Longevity and Balance:
- Sustainable wealth is about building a financial foundation that lasts for your lifetime and can even support future generations. The five-fold millionaire approach emphasizes the need for balance in life. By ensuring that each area—spiritual, mental, emotional, physical, and financial—grows

together, you can avoid burnout and achieve true fulfillment.

- This balance promotes long-term well-being because concentrating only on finances while neglecting your health or emotional wellness can lead to burnout and poor decision-making. This, in turn, can undermine your financial success.

3. Building Multiple Streams of Wealth:
- A five-fold millionaire doesn't just focus on growing their financial assets; they also nurture other forms of wealth, like relationships (emotional wealth), health (physical wealth), and personal fulfillment (spiritual wealth). Similarly, sustainable wealth relies on diversification—not only in financial investments but also across different areas of life. This approach helps create resilience and reduces dependency on any single source of wealth.

For example, investing in your physical health gives you the energy and stamina to enjoy your financial gains, while taking care of your mental well-being helps you make smart financial decisions and grab new opportunities when they arise.

4. Legacy and Impact:
- Sustainable wealth includes the idea of **leaving a lasting legacy**, whether through financial inheritance, philanthropy, or positive societal contributions. The five-fold millionaire concept expands on this by incorporating the idea of **legacy-building across all dimensions** of wealth, including leaving behind emotional stability, wisdom, and spiritual fulfillment for future generations.
- This connection to legacy means that both sustainable wealth and five-fold wealth are **future-focused**—not just accumulating resources for the present, but creating systems and

practices that ensure long-term benefits for your family, community, or society.

5. Purpose and Fulfillment:
- Sustainable wealth aligns with the **spiritual** and **mental** aspects of the five-fold millionaire, as it stresses the importance of finding purpose and fulfillment in what you do with your wealth. Instead of pursuing wealth solely for material gain, both approaches emphasize the need to align wealth-building with your life's purpose and core values.

- When your **spiritual wealth** is intact, the financial wealth becomes a tool to further your mission, support causes you believe in, and contribute to personal and community growth, leading to greater fulfillment.

6. Continual Growth and Learning:
- A five-fold millionaire understands the importance of ongoing personal and professional growth in every area of

life, just as sustainable wealth calls for continuous learning and adaptation to market conditions, economic shifts, and life changes.

- This commitment to continuous growth ensures you're not stagnant in any aspect of your life, whether it's financial investments, personal relationships, or health. It reinforces the sustainability of your wealth, as you're always evolving and making improvements to promote longevity and stability.

7. Mindset and Perspective:
- Both sustainable wealth and the five-fold millionaire require a **shift in mindset**—away from short-term gains or single-dimensional thinking and towards a **comprehensive, long-term perspective**. The five-fold millionaire embraces the understanding that true wealth requires nurturing all dimensions of life, which is also a key principle of sustainable wealth.

- This mindset of abundance is critical in ensuring that wealth isn't just about accumulating financial resources but about creating **lasting prosperity** that permeates every aspect of your life.

Sustainable wealth and the idea of a **five-fold millionaire** are two sides of the same coin. Both advocate for a comprehensive approach to wealth, focusing on balance, longevity, and the nurturing of multiple areas of life. Together, they create a roadmap for building wealth that is not only financially sound but also spiritually, emotionally, mentally, and physically enriching, ensuring true prosperity that endures and empowers future generations.

Wealth that Endures: The Five-Fold Millionaire's
Guide to Lasting Abundance

Chapter 3
How Can I Build Sustainable Wealth?

As a five-fold millionaire, building sustainable wealth means leveraging your approach to wealth across **spiritual, mental, emotional, physical, and financial** dimensions in a way that ensures long-term stability and growth. Here's how you can achieve that:

1. **Spiritual Wealth: Aligning Purpose with Prosperity**
   - **Stay Grounded in Your Values**: Sustainable wealth begins with a clear sense of purpose. Make sure your wealth-building strategies align with

your spiritual beliefs and values. When your financial pursuits are in harmony with your purpose, you create wealth that feels meaningful and fulfilling.

- **Give Back and Serve**: Building wealth sustainably includes contributing to causes or communities that resonate with your values. Whether through philanthropy, mentorship, or other forms of giving, channeling part of your wealth into helping others fosters a sense of spiritual abundance and deepens your sense of purpose.

2. **Mental Wealth: Continuous Learning and Growth**
   - **Invest in Knowledge**: Mental wealth is about sharpening your mind and staying informed about the markets, investments, and new opportunities. Continuously educate yourself on emerging trends, financial strategies, and industries that align with your goals.

- **Adaptability**: Building sustainable wealth means staying flexible. The world of business and finance is always changing, so being mentally prepared to adapt ensures that you can pivot when needed and take advantage of new opportunities that support long-term growth.

3. **Emotional Wealth: Building Strong Relationships and Emotional Resilience**
    - **Nurture Relationships**: Surround yourself with a strong support system of family, friends, mentors, and business partners who uplift and motivate you. Emotional wealth grows when you invest in relationships that support your vision, and these connections can open doors to new financial opportunities and collaborations.
    - **Emotional Intelligence in Decision Making**: Your emotional state impacts the decisions you make with your

wealth. Cultivate emotional resilience by managing stress and practicing mindfulness. This ensures that your financial decisions are grounded in logic and clarity, helping you avoid impulsive or reactive choices that could jeopardize your wealth.

4. **Physical Wealth: Health as a Foundation for Longevity**
   - **Prioritize Physical Health**: Sustainable wealth isn't just about money—it's also about having the energy, vitality, and longevity to enjoy it. Investing in your physical well-being through exercise, nutrition, and wellness practices ensures that you have the stamina to pursue your goals for the long term.
   - **Create a Healthy Environment**: Surround yourself with habits and environments that promote physical health, such as minimizing stress, getting enough rest, and taking care of your mental well-being. Good health is

a foundation for maintaining the drive and clarity needed to manage your wealth.

5. **Financial Wealth: Building Lasting Financial Security**
   - **Diversify Investments**: Ensure your financial wealth is sustainable by diversifying your portfolio. This includes a mix of stocks, bonds, real estate, business ventures, and other assets that provide multiple streams of income. Diversification reduces risk and helps you weather financial downturns.

   - **Focus on Cash Flow and Passive Income**: Develop streams of **passive income**—such as rental properties, dividends, or royalties—that allow your wealth to grow even when you're not actively working. Having consistent, reliable cash flow ensures that you maintain financial stability.

- **Manage Debt and Build a Safety Net**: Minimize unnecessary debt, and be strategic about leveraging credit for investments that will appreciate over time. Additionally, build an emergency fund or financial safety net to protect your wealth during difficult times, ensuring its longevity.

- **Tax Efficiency and Estate Planning**: Part of sustainable financial wealth is ensuring that you keep more of what you earn. Work with financial advisors to implement tax-efficient strategies and engage in proper estate planning to preserve your wealth for future generations.

6. **Legacy and Impact: Long-Term Wealth for Future Generations**
    - **Build a Legacy Plan**: Think about how your wealth will benefit not only yourself but also your family and community. Create an estate plan, trusts, or foundations to ensure that your financial wealth supports future

generations and leaves a lasting impact.

- **Educate Heirs and Successors**: Sustainable wealth isn't just about passing on money; it's about passing on knowledge and values. Educate your children, heirs, or business successors on financial literacy and wealth management to ensure they can continue building on the legacy you've created.

By focusing on all these dimensions of wealth as a five-fold millionaire, you can build a sustainable, lasting form of prosperity that will not only grow over time but also provide fulfillment and stability in every area of your life. This integrated approach ensures that your wealth is resilient and adaptable to change, while supporting your personal growth and the well-being of future generations.

Wealth that Endures: The Five-Fold Millionaire's
Guide to Lasting Abundance

Chapter 4
Mindset and Attitude

The right mindset and attitude are crucial for a five-fold millionaire and for building sustainable wealth. It all starts with how you think about money and success. A growth mindset is key—it's the belief that you can improve and learn from your experiences. This kind of thinking helps you see challenges as opportunities rather than obstacles. When you embrace a growth mindset, you're more likely to take risks, learn from your mistakes, and keep pushing forward.

Resilience is another important piece of the puzzle. Life is full of ups and downs, and there will be times when things don't go as planned. Being resilient means, you bounce back from setbacks and keep your eyes on your goals. It's about not letting failures define you but rather using them as steppingstones to success.

Adapting to change is equally essential. The world around us is always shifting economies fluctuate, industries evolve, and personal circumstances can change in an instant. Those who thrive are the ones who can pivot and adjust their strategies when needed. Instead of resisting change, embrace it. Look for ways to innovate and improve, whether in your financial strategies or your personal growth.

By cultivating a positive mindset, fostering resilience, and being open to change, you lay a solid foundation for sustainable wealth. This mindset will not only help you grow your financial assets but also enrich your life in every area, aligning perfectly with the five-fold millionaire approach. Remember, it's not just about the destination; it's about how you navigate the journey.

Your attitude truly shapes your altitude when it comes to building and sustaining wealth. Think of it this way: your attitude is like the lens through which you view your financial journey. If you approach wealth with a positive, open-minded attitude, you're more likely to see opportunities where others might see obstacles.

A can-do attitude encourages you to take initiative and seek solutions rather than getting bogged down by challenges. When you believe in your ability to learn and grow, you're more inclined to take calculated risks and make bold moves, which can lead to greater financial rewards.

On the flip side, a negative attitude can hold you back. If you focus on fear, self-doubt, or a scarcity mindset, you might miss out on opportunities or avoid taking necessary steps to grow your wealth. When you're constantly worried about what could go wrong, it can paralyze your decision-making and keep you from taking action.

Moreover, your attitude affects how you handle setbacks. Everyone faces challenges on their wealth-building journey, but those with a resilient and optimistic mindset are more likely to bounce back, learn from their mistakes, and keep pushing forward. They see failures as temporary hurdles, not roadblocks.

In essence, your attitude sets the tone for your financial journey. A positive, growth-oriented attitude will lift you higher, allowing you to build and sustain wealth effectively. It's about believing in yourself, staying motivated, and keeping your eyes on the prize, no matter what challenges come your way.

Chapter 5
Building Wealth 1$ at a Time

My husband and I are both self-employed and knew that one day we would have to retire. We knew that social security would not be sufficient to keep us comfortable. That is when we decided to invest, save, and live a debt free as possible.

Our goals was to develop multiple streams of income. Through his furniture restoration business, he was able to develop several streams of income within the business. With my income tax and accounting, and perfume manufacturing businesses I was able to develop multiple streams of income so that no matter what happened economically, we could sustain our lifestyle.

Next, we retired as much debt as possible. Starting with paying off cars, credit cards and any other debt that we deemed necessary.

Our next step was to look at investment sources such as certificates of deposit, savings, stocks, and retirement accounts. We were able to leverage all of these into a comfortable portfolio.

Four main reasons we have been able to accomplish this:

1. We learned to live below our means. We never spend excessively. We still enjoy trips and other luxuries while still living below our means.

2. We purposed to always set money aside into our various accounts.

3. We live a life of generosity and Stewardship, servanthood to the Kingdom of God.

4. If it doesn't fit the budget, then we won't do it.

Addressing strategy #1, *learning to live below your means*, is crucial because it lays the foundation for sustainable wealth building. This strategy is about more than just frugality; it's a mindset shift that prioritizes financial health and long-term security over immediate gratification.

When you commit to living below your means, you create a buffer between your income and your expenses. This allows you to save and invest more, providing a safety net for unexpected challenges and opportunities. For example, when you spend less than you earn, you can allocate extra funds toward savings, retirement accounts, or investments, which are essential for growing your wealth over time.

Additionally, living below your means fosters financial discipline. It encourages you to be intentional with your spending, helping you distinguish between needs and wants. This awareness can lead to better financial decisions, reducing the temptation to overspend or rely on credit.

Ultimately, this strategy not only helps you build wealth but also promotes peace of mind. By living below your means, you reduce financial stress, allowing you to focus on your goals and enjoy life without the burden of debt or financial anxiety. It's a powerful step toward achieving and sustaining wealth in the long run.

"Living below your means" simply means spending less money than you earn. It's about making conscious choices to prioritize your financial health over immediate wants or desires.

For example, if you earn $3,000 a month, living below your means might mean only spending $2,500. This way, you have an extra $500 to save, invest, or use to pay off debt.

It often involves budgeting, avoiding unnecessary expenses, and being mindful about how you use your money. By living below your means, you can build savings, reduce financial stress, and create a more secure future. Essentially, it's about finding a balance that allows you to enjoy life while still planning for tomorrow.

Wealth that Endures: The Five-Fold Millionaire's Guide to Lasting Abundance

Chapter 6
Practical Steps

I like to include practical steps to guide my readers along the way. I find that practical application is the only way to ensure that we reach our goals through the disciplines found in these steps.

Here's a checklist of practical steps you can follow to start building sustainable wealth:

1. Create a Budget
- **Track Your Income and Expenses**: Use apps like Mint or YNAB to see where your money goes. This will go a long way in helping you determine what expenses are draining your money.

- **Set Spending Limits**: Allocate specific amounts for essential categories (housing, food, transportation) and discretionary spending.

2. **Build an Emergency Fund**
   - **Save 3-6 Months of Expenses**: Aim to have a cushion that covers your living expenses for a few months in case of unexpected events.
   - **Automate Savings**: Set up automatic transfers to your savings account each month.

3. **Cut Unnecessary Expenses**
   - **Review Subscriptions**: Cancel any subscriptions or memberships you no longer use. You would be surprised how subscriptions or memberships can add up and drain your money. Think of it this way, this is money you could be saving for a rainy day.
   - **Limit Dining Out**: Plan meals at home and set a budget for dining out.

4. Pay Off Debt

- **List Your Debts**: Write down all your debts, interest rates, and minimum payments.

- **Create a Repayment Plan**: Consider the debt snowball (paying off smaller debts first) or avalanche (paying off high-interest debts first) methods.

5. Invest Wisely

- **Start with Retirement Accounts**: Contribute to a 401(k) or IRA for tax benefits and long-term growth.

- **Consider Low-Cost Index Funds**: These can provide diversified exposure to the stock market with lower fees.

6. Diversify Your Income

- **Explore Side Hustles**: Consider freelance work, consulting, or selling products online. My book, *Developing Multiple Streams of Income*, will provide readers with valuable ideas on how to create additional income streams, which is key to building and sustaining wealth. This will further equip them on their journey toward achieving financial independence and long-term security.

- **Invest in Skills**: Take courses or workshops to enhance your skills, making you more valuable in the job market.

7. Educate Yourself

- **Read Books and Articles**: Dive into personal finance literature to broaden your knowledge.

- **Follow Financial Experts**: Subscribe to podcasts, blogs, or social media channels that offer valuable insights on wealth building.

8. Practice Self-Care

- **Prioritize Health and Wellness**: Regular exercise, healthy eating, and sufficient sleep can boost productivity and decision-making.

- **Manage Stress**: Engage in activities that promote relaxation, such as meditation, yoga, or hobbies you enjoy. Self-care is vital to your overall wealth balance. You are a five-fold millionaire and balance is your portion.

9. Set Long-Term Goals
- **Define Your Financial Goals**: Think about what you want to achieve in the next 5, 10, or 20 years (buying a home, retiring early, etc.). Revisit *The Five-Fold Millionaire* as you begin to define your goals.

- **Create a Vision Board**: Visualizing your goals can keep you motivated and focused on your path to wealth. You can find vision board examples on the internet.

10. Review and Adjust Regularly
- **Check Your Progress**: Review your budget, savings, and investments regularly to ensure you're on track.

- **Make Adjustments as Needed**: Life changes, and so should your financial strategies. Be flexible and willing to adapt.

By following these actionable steps, you can take meaningful strides toward building and sustaining your wealth, creating a solid foundation for your financial future.

Chapter 7
Time to Move Forward and Build Wealth

We have come to the conclusion of this little book, but I hope that combined with the *Five-Fold Millionaire: Walking in Your Wealthy Place*, you now have the tools necessary to walk into your wealthy place.

Wealth building won't happen overnight, and it won't always be easy, but it is possible. Free your mind and your wealth will follow.

Don't allow your past to shape the way you move forward. Growth is a process so don't despise the process.

As you embark on your journey toward sustainable wealth and embrace the principles of the five-fold millionaire, remember that true prosperity goes beyond just financial success—it encompasses your spirit, mind, body, and relationships. By committing to live below your means, investing in yourself, and nurturing all aspects of your life, you can create a legacy that not only enriches your own life but also positively impacts those around you. So, take the first step today, cultivate your mindset, and let your aspirations guide you toward a life of abundance, fulfillment, and lasting success. You have the power to shape your financial future—now is the time to seize it!

Be Blessed!

ABOUT THE AUTHOR

Genuine leadership is found amongst those audacious enough to signal the importance of others to the rest of the world. Trailblazing a path where philanthropy meets world class ingenuity; is the compassionate professional; Dr. Jacquie Hadnot.

Dr. Jacquie is a 32-time best-selling author, filmmaker, producer, cleric, and dedicated entrepreneur who founded Mallie Boushaye Essentials and Fragrances by Mallie Boushaye. Proficient in creating distinctive conglomerates, Dr. Hadnot has skillfully maintained a six-figure manufacturing and retail business while steadfastly adhering to her life's core purpose — inspiring, empowering, and encouraging people. Renowned for her exceptional ability to alter perspectives, instill purpose, and effect change in a diverse clientele, Jacquie continues to be a highly sought-after advocate in the realms of business, ministry, and social spheres.

Dr. Jacquie combines unyielding excellence with a sincere regard for education, achievement, and community involvement. She holds a PhD in Pastoral Theology, MA in Leadership, BA in Theology, and a degree in Accounting. In accommodation to her propensity for educational acumen, she has also attained certifications in life, business, and cancer care coaching. Her contributions in vocation, workshop facilitation, and ministerial advancements are awe-inspiring; as she has not only managed to lead in sales and ethics, but also in creating quintessential forms of humanitarianism, including support groups and multi-dimensional outreach programs. Dr. Jacquie's serviceability has proven highly prolific, as she was 2022 recipient of the Joe Biden Presidential Lifetime Achievement Award; easily yielding her one of the most effective leaders of our time.

Whether she is coaching the masses, empowering entrepreneurs, or overseeing her own business enterprises, Dr. Jacquie displays no corroboration in slowing down. When she is not out leaving a lasting impression on the world, she is an asset to her local communal body, and a loving member of her family and friendship circles.

Wealth that Endures: The Five-Fold Millionaire's
Guide to Lasting Abundance

Other Books & Materials by Dr. Jacquie

- Another Famine in the Land (Oct 2023)
- Art of Spiritual Warfare: Strategies for Warfare
- Art of Spiritual Warfare: Strategies for Warfare: Study Guide
- Art of Spiritual Warfare: Breaking Soul Ties That Bind
- Art of Spiritual Warfare: Taking Authority Over Your Spiritual House
- Art of Spiritual Warfare: Confessions of a Warrior
- Art of Spiritual Warfare: Journal
- Art of Spiritual Warfare: Breaking Soul Ties the Bind
- Art of Spiritual Warfare: Demolishing Poverty Spirit
- Art of Spiritual Warfare: Destroying Spiritual Breaches
- Art of Spiritual Warfare: Demon Hit List
- Art of Spiritual Warfare: Idols Must Fall
- Art of Spiritual Warfare: Warfare of Prayer
- Art of Spiritual Warfare: Prayers for Effective Warfare
- Art of Spiritual Warfare in the Marketplace
- Art of Spiritual Warfare: Para Bellum
- Audacious Prayer, Audacious Pursuit, Audacious Power
- A Treasure in the Pleasure of Loving God
- A Woman of Worth: Loving the Skin I'm In
- A Woman of Worth: Loving the Skin I'm In Study Guide
- A Woman of Worth: From Victim to Victor
- A Woman of Worth: Dressed to Heal (Book & Journal)
- A Woman of Worth: Talitha Cumi, Woman Arise!
- A Woman of Worth: I Hope You Dance
- Affirmations for a Woman of Worth Study Guide
- A Woman of Worth: I Am More Than Enough
- Blood on the Wall: From Trauma to Triumph
- Catching Hell On Another Became My Blessing
- Closing the Doors to Satan's Attacks: Overcoming Fear

Wealth that Endures: The Five-Fold Millionaire's Guide to Lasting Abundance

- Crushed and Poured Out: Pour My Oil On Your Feet
- Cry Aloud, Spare Not! A Prophetic Call to the Fast
- Cry Aloud, Spare Not! The Companion-Study Guide
- Deeper…
- Developing Multiple Streams of Income
- Diamonds & Orchids
- Don't Despise the Process: Strategies for Healing
- Don't Despise the Process: Learning to Live
- Enemy in Me: Overcoming Self-Life Issues
- Extravagant Love of God: Experiencing Prophetic Flow
- Five-Fold Millionaire: Walking in Your Wealthy Place
- Five-Fold Millionaire: Interactive Study Guide
- Forty Days for Your Soul: My Souls Follows Hard
- Front Line Woman: Warriors, Disciples & Over Comers
- His Mercy Endures Forever: Psalms, Prayers
- Ignite My Fire, Lord (Book & Journal)
- In the Face of Adversity: Overcoming Life's Storms
- Kingdom Authority: Missions, Mantles, and Mandates
- Loving God through His Names: 365 Days of the Year
- Naked, Broken and Unashamed
- Pretty in Pink: Praying Influential Nonsense Free Women
- Standing for the King: While in Spotlight of the Media
- There's a Famine in the Land: Overcoming the Great Recession
- Time to Write That Book: Where Do I Begin?
- To Make War with the Saints: Satan's Kingdom Agenda
- Trapped in the Arms of Death: Overcoming Suicide
- Unlocking the Power to Get Wealth
- Where Is Your God? Have We Lost the Fear of the Lord?
- Your Declaration of Dependence on God
- When Fear Crept In

Prophetic Flow - CD
- More of You… (Volume 1)
- Healing Prayers

Wealth that Endures: The Five-Fold Millionaire's Guide to Lasting Abundance

Audio Books & Teachings
- In the Face of Adversity: Overcoming Life's Storms
- Be Not Deceived…
- Where Is Your God?
- Recognizing Your Due Season
- Praying the Healing Scriptures
- The Enemy in Me: Overcoming Self-Life Issues
- Trusting God in a Season of Discouragement
- The Harlot Heart

Journals
- Be Still and Know that I am God
- More of You
- Diary of a Psalmist

Music
- Who Am I? Woman of Worth
- The Extravagant Love of God
- The Spoken Word of Love
- His Mercy Endures Forever: Praying the Psalms

DVD
- Unlocking the Power to Create Wealth
- Unlocking the Power to Create Wealth: Dimensions of Power
- When Your Faith is Being Tested
- What Made David Run
- Agents of Change
- Virtuous Women of Worship
- Secrets of the Secret Place: Dwelling Place
- Secrets of the Secret Place: Renewing Your Strength
- Secrets of the Secret Place: Prayer Key to Kingdom
- Secrets of the Secret Place: Rest & Believe

Wealth that Endures: The Five-Fold Millionaire's
Guide to Lasting Abundance

Anthology Collaborations
- Reset and Relaunch
- Coat of May Colors
- Greatness In You Anthology with Les Brown
- Igniting the World With Our Voices
- Prioritizing My Battles: I Can't Afford to Fight You Too
- Women of Power Ignited to Serve
- Trapped Behind Enemy Lines In My Mind
- Prisoner of War in the Mind

Wealth that Endures: The Five-Fold Millionaire's Guide to Lasting Abundance

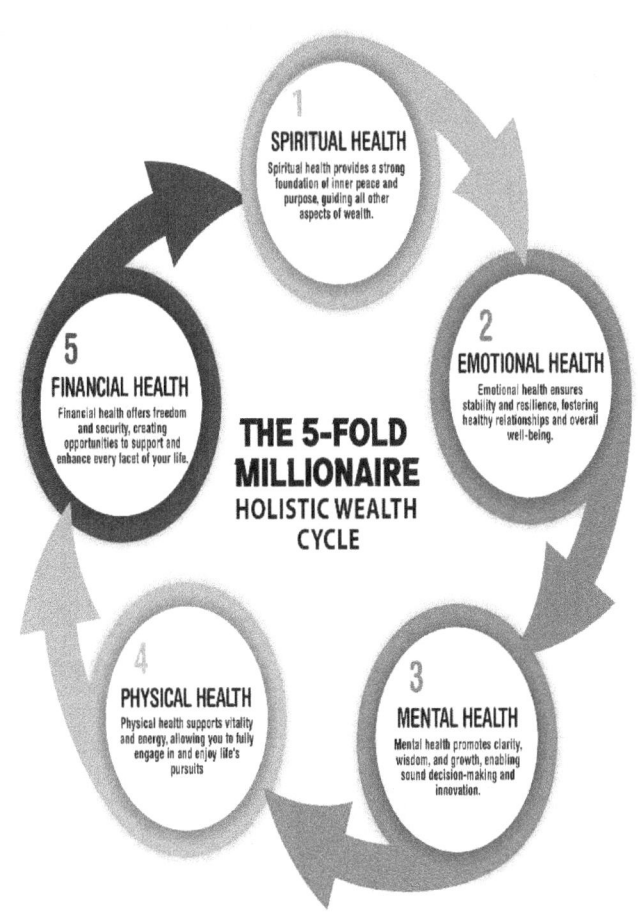

THE FIVE-FOLD MILLIONAIRE
WALKING IN YOUR WEALTHY PLACE
DR. JACQUELYN HADNOT
ALL RIGHTS RESERVED

Wealth that Endures: The Five-Fold Millionaire's
Guide to Lasting Abundance

www.ingramcontent.com/pod-product-compliance
Lightning Source LLC
Chambersburg PA
CBHW030051230526
45471CB00003B/1045